You Could Have It All

You Could Have It All

Geoffrey Thomas

Reformation Heritage Books
Grand Rapids, Michigan

You Could Have It All
© 2020 by Geoffrey Thomas

Reformation Heritage Books
2965 Leonard St. NE
Grand Rapids, MI 49525
616-977-0889
orders@heritagebooks.org
www.heritagebooks.org

Printed in the United States of America
20 21 22 23 24 25/10 9 8 7 6 5 4 3 2

Library of Congress Cataloging-in-Publication Data

Names: Thomas, Geoff, 1938- author.
Title: You could have it all / Geoffrey Thomas.
Description: Grand Rapids, Michigan : Reformation Heritage Books,
    2020.
Identifiers: LCCN 2020013414 (print) | LCCN 2020013415 (ebook) |
    ISBN 9781601787927 (paperback) | ISBN 9781601787934 (epub)
Subjects: LCSH: Christianity—Essence, genius, nature. | Trust in
    God—Christianity.
Classification: LCC BT60 .T46 2020 (print) | LCC BT60 (ebook) |
    DDC 234/.2—dc23
LC record available at https://lccn.loc.gov/2020013414
LC ebook record available at https://lccn.loc.gov/2020013415

*For additional Reformed literature, request a free book list from
Reformation Heritage Books at the above regular or email address.*

These things did these three mighty men.
—2 SAMUEL 23:17

❧

Gary Brady, Glyn Ellis, Ian Alsop
a pastor, an elder, and a deacon

They loved the Lord Jesus Christ.
They loved the grace of God.
They loved and served the church of Jesus Christ.
They loved and married my three daughters.
They nurtured and cared for my nine grandchildren.
They have become my most esteemed friends
  and eternal brothers.

Contents

You Could Have It All!

What am I talking about? Knowing the purpose and meaning of life and maintaining that vision day by day; experiencing lasting joy and peace; having that precious knowledge of oneself; finding fulfillment; experiencing lasting, rich relationships; having hope in death; receiving knowledge of the God who is the Creator of the cosmos: you really could have all that.

"Ah, I see. This is about religion, isn't it?" Please! Pause a moment before you simply dismiss this, before you refuse to consider even another word, let alone a sentence. Don't slip immediately into your automatic rejection of religion. Don't allow such prejudice to control you. Perhaps you've thought about religion in the past. You may have tried religion when you were younger, or maybe you've been let down by religions or religious people. That's not unlikely. Millions of people have. I am not very interested in religions myself. Some of them are mankind's greatest crimes. I'll be absolutely truthful with you: I am more interested in a certain remarkable person—Jesus Christ.

Don't switch off, please, even if it's unusual for you to be reading a religious book. Shouldn't there be a set time or two in every rational and inquiring person's life when he or she spares a thought for the preacher of the Sermon on the Mount, the one whom every Christian claims to be more powerful than death? I acknowledge that these pages are about Him. I believe that divine providence has put this little book into your hands in some strange way.

Having it all—getting the very best anyone can get in life—is, in my conviction, being gripped by the most remarkable person in the history of the world. Have you ever considered Him? He is extraordinary. Think of it: Jesus had meekness without weakness, tenderness without feebleness, firmness without belligerence, straight speaking without coarseness, love without sentimentality, righteousness without being sanctimonious, truth without error, zeal without fanaticism, passion without prejudice, heavenly-mindedness without unreality, service without servility, convictions without egotism, evaluation without prejudice, love for Himself while loving His neighbors as Himself, beauty without vanity, joy without any depression. How extraordinary that such a man has made Himself open to inspection in our cynical world! Such a character and personality that anyone with any sense would admire is found in this man. We are persuaded that He is God's great definition of a proper man, the archetypal man, the altogether strong and lovely man. He is the one who is offering men and women everything they need for a blessed life now and lasting joy and peace forevermore.

Now you might be tempted to think another reluctant thought: "OK, well, maybe I'll give religion a try." No! I don't want you to consider that as an option, as if you can get a sample of everything you need in life by briefly putting your toe in the water and then taking it out and deciding it's not for you. It can't be like that in order to have it all. Having it all, I say, isn't based on some temporary hunch, like "I'll give religion a shot." Why not? Because if it is as easy as that, then whenever the going gets tough—and there are hard decisions to be made—you'd leave this religion phase immediately with a measure of relief, looking very serious and saying quietly with all the conviction you could muster, "Yes, I have tried religion. Been there, done that. It's OK for some, but not for me."

You can have it all only by the grace of Jesus Christ: only because of the tender, loving-kindness of the Son of God homing in on you, capturing your interest, answering your inner objections. You are still reading these words because God has been working with you and in you, maybe over many years. He is the One who has been enriching your life.

I am convinced that nothing has ever happened to you or me because of mere luck, chance, or fate. The best things we've enjoyed in life—loving parents, a dear wife or husband, precious children, health and long life, employment and prosperity—have all been the gifts of God. And the worst things in this groaning and fallen world did not occur because God was looking away. God is always in control of our lives, even when the news is the worst. The fact that somehow you got hold of this piece of literature and are still reading these words is significant. I believe this mild curiosity has been planted in your mind by God, not by my fascinating turn of phrase, or by the heavy heart you have from some wretched business deal or personal loss over the past weeks, or by a breakdown in what had been a precious relationship. It is not just a time of vulnerability that is making you go against your long-held conviction that you're not a religious person. You may now be stumbling across ultimate reality, confronting the truth that the God of love lives and that He acts and is in charge of your life at this very moment. You may have a growing realization that this God has not given up on you, even though you may have neglected Him for decades.

This is actually the set time for you to know that a life of emptiness and shattering disappointments is in fact an utterly unnatural life. It should not be like this, and it need not go on in this way. It can and must be changed. You could have all that is in the power of the loving-kindness of your Creator to give to you, not because you have earned it but simply because God loves you. Remember, He is the One who lies behind this unexpected event, that you, who have gone on for years without good thoughts of Jesus Christ, should continue to read these sentences and reconsider what it tells you of how you could have it all.

I have tried to disabuse you of the idea that religion is something you may briefly pick up and then throw aside at a whim. You are not in charge of what is happening. All you are now experiencing has been ordained before there was light. God is motivating you to continue reading. He is in charge of this encounter, and as the God of measureless love He alone can make someone a lover of Himself. The events leading to your taking up this book—whether through the providence of sheer discovery or perhaps through a person you know and admire—are the gifts of a loving God. And your openness to tiptoe into this barely visited territory—to think again about the issues I am raising— is also one of the ways God helps men and women He loves to discover the purpose of their lives and how they can have everything that's needed for a life of joy and peace. Why do we exist? What are we here for? Can man know God? My sentences in this little book seek to be as important as those questions. It is worthwhile considering these things if it will result in your having it all. You have not been so successful in your quest so far, have you?

Of course you have every right to question whether I am some sort of fanatic to be addressing you in this way. Am I another muddled and deluded man who is rubbing your conscience and tormenting you with my foolish words? If so, you have every right to stop reading this right now. But if what you are reading and will continue to read is true—that it is possible for us to learn what life is all about and to receive from God all we need for a lifetime's enjoyment and fulfillment— then let me go on to tell you as clearly as I can how you really can have it all. Let's start.

ONE

You Could Know God

The greatest proof for the existence of God is the Lord Jesus Christ. This brave young teacher stirred up the Middle East as He spoke to growing crowds of people while traveling through His little nation. We learn of five thousand men following Him for miles and sitting down to listen to Him, and such large crowds were not unusual for Him. After three years, His life and teaching had been so effective that more than five hundred people had become His disciples. Soon another three thousand began to serve Him, a number that grew to five thousand, all believing that He was who He claimed to be: the Son of God and the only way to God. He drew people to Himself. The picture we find in the gospels is of vast audiences hanging onto His words, which continued for almost three years until He was killed. Before dawn broke, people could be found sitting around the place He was staying, waiting for Him to open the front door and make an appearance, wanting to get help from Him, having failed to get it from anywhere or anyone

else. His teaching was frequently profound and pro-
vocative. He never quoted the historic teachers of the
previous two hundred years in order to hide His beliefs
behind their views. He spoke on His own authority and
was prepared to challenge what earlier religious leaders
had said, often disdaining and correcting widely held
theories about religious practices that destroyed natural
affection and the law of God.

Christ frequently quoted from the Old Testament
Scriptures, prefacing His remarks by the words "It is
written." He never contradicted the Bible—a fact of no
small significance. The God who had often spoken in
the past by His servants the prophets now appeared in
the form of His Son, Jesus. He spoke face-to-face with
individuals, mothers, children, fishermen, cynics, soldiers, and tax officials.

With a wonderful cogency, Jesus spoke unforget-
table aphorisms such as "The Son of Man came to seek
and to save those who are lost.... What will it profit a
man if he were to gain the whole world and lose his
own soul?... I came not to be served but to serve and to
give my life a ransom for many.... Give to Caesar the
things that are Caesar's, but to God the things that are
God's.... Father, forgive them; for they know not what
they do.... Blessed are the pure in heart: for they shall
see God." No one else ever spoke like this man.

The Lord Jesus Christ also made the most staggering claims. He said that on a future day He would
judge the whole world, that all men and women would
have to give an account to Him and would receive their

destinies from His lips. We live in a moral universe in which our actions and words count. They are powerful to help or to hurt others, and what we are sowing by the influence of our actions and words is what we are going to reap. There lies before mankind a great day of evaluation that will result in approval and vindication for many, and just and fair condemnation for others. Jesus said He would be the one discriminating and judging us in that day. What a claim to make to people who had known Him and His mother very well. He had helped Mary's husband for years, making posts, window frames, tables, and cupboards, yet now He also claims that He is going to pass judgment on the whole of mankind. Some had seen Him grow up from infancy to boyhood to adolescence to full manhood; now He made these staggering statements, that to Him we will all have to give account in a future day of cosmic evaluation.

But He claims more than that. The criterion by which He will make His judgments will be how we related to Him. Did we serve Him, honor Him, and speak well of Him, or were we rather ashamed of Him? He told His hearers that many would be claiming they'd been serving Him, but He would tell them that He never knew them. That would be the key for entering an eternal life of blessedness with Him: being loved by Him and being recognized as those He knew and had delighted in.

There is nothing ordinary about someone who tells the whole world they are all going to give an account to Him and hear of their destinies from His lips. Is this man a lunatic? Is He wicked to make such staggering claims? For example, He says that no one can approach God except by the Lord Christ. He is the only Mediator who can reconcile fallen man with a perfectly holy God. Those are some of the claims of Jesus of Galilee. Who can speak like this? Who has the right to make these claims and be taken seriously? Simply a person of majestic righteousness and love, who always spoke the truth.

But more than this, the Lord Jesus Christ claimed preexistence. He once said, "Before Abraham was, I am." The rest of mankind all began at conception. We had no existence before that, but He goes back to before the beginning of time. John's gospel begins with these awesome words: "In the beginning was the Word, and the Word was with God, and the Word was God. The same was in the beginning with God." He is different from any of us.

Jesus Christ also claimed absolute deity. He claimed to be God, saying, "I and my Father are one." When one of His disciples fell before Him and whispered in broken worship, "My Lord and my God" after He had risen from the dead, Jesus didn't shake His head and say, "Tut, tut! We can't have any of that blasphemy. Don't go setting me up on a pedestal. I'm just on ordinary guy." There is nothing ordinary about a man whom the wind and waves obeyed. This world has witnessed a man as pure and holy as God, someone more powerful than death. This world has witnessed someone who practiced what He preached to others. "Love your enemies.... Pray for them which despitefully use you," He said, and then when they nailed Him to a cross and lifted Him up to die in indescribable torment, He prayed for them, "Father, forgive them; for they know not what they do." Those are some of the most godlike words ever spoken.

Jesus Christ is scarcely a crazy man or megalomaniac. He is surely the most sane individual the world has ever seen. He is not an evil man or consummate liar responsible for deceiving countless numbers of both sophisticated and simple people from Galilee to the Silicon Valley of California. If not wicked or insane, then what? He is the incarnate God who spoke through His servants the prophets from Moses until the first century, and now He comes very close, making Himself known to us in His Son, Jesus Christ.

TWO

You Could Know Yourself

What's life all about? Who am I and why do I exist? There might have been times when you asked yourself those questions. Maybe it was at 3 a.m. on a sleepless night when everything seemed to be falling apart. Once on the *Muppet Show* the late Peter Sellers was being interviewed by Kermit the Frog. The conversation began with the speaker in charge of the puppet seeking to put the comedian-actor at ease, saying, "Now, Peter, just relax and be yourself." Sellers shook his head at the puppet, saying soberly, "I can't be myself because I don't know who I am. The real me doesn't exist."

If you're seeking to discover who you are by contemplating the whole of the cosmos, you'll reach the inevitable truth that men and women are the tiniest of tiny specks. That's not at all comforting to think that everything is incomprehensively vast and we are so insignificantly tiny.

Or you might seek your identity in the animal world, comparing yourself, for example, to a monkey in the primate family. But does that provide you with any more wisdom, to conclude that maybe all you are is a mere naked ape? How vast the gulf between that world and humankind. We would certainly pay a lot to hear a performance of Vaughan Williams's *The Lark Ascending*, but we are most unlikely to spend any money to purchase a ticket to enter the Albert Hall to hear an actual lark's song. A dish of food is placed before an animal, and it devours it. If it's a bowl of water, the animal slakes its thirst. You put a mate before it and it copulates. You put a weaker enemy before it, and it will attack and kill. There is this vast gulf between man and the humbler creation. We are not like animals, and we don't want to behave as they do. We know such graces as self-sacrifice, restraint, modesty, self-denial, mercy, and justice. We also have a sense of beauty and creativity. The great gulf between Shakespeare, da Vinci, Churchill, Dickens, Beethoven, and Mandela and the whole zoological world is so vast as to be totally uncrossable. Of course, there are some likenesses, such as the design of an animal's heart or its nervous system. The valve of a sheep's or a pig's heart can be transplanted to a human being. They are of identical design. But little explanation is coming from the animal world to explain how a man would choose to lay down his life so that others might be spared. Many have done so. A man called Stephen was being stoned to death by a mob baying for his blood, and he prayed for them, under that hail of jagged rocks breaking his ribs and skull, that God would not lay this cruelty to their charge. He took their responsibility in killing him very seriously (they would answer to God for it), but he also took his responsibility seriously in pleading with God to show them mercy, having received such mercy himself.

To discover who and what you are, you must look to the God who has made Himself known to the world in Jesus Christ. In the opening chapters of the Bible, we learn that when God had concluded creating the first man He looked at His handiwork and what was before Him as His own likeness, just as you look in a mirror and see the image of yourself accurately reflected. In the beginning there was no disharmony or estrangement between God and mankind. No murderers, rapists, tyrants, or crooked businessmen walked the earth in Eden. There was a time of spontaneous affection and trust when God and man walked in harmony. It was a time of probation and testing, but man was dissatisfied to be under so transcendent and magnificent a being. He thought he knew better than God. Many still do. Man listened to the lies of a dark power, and so unspeakable iniquity and death came into the world and still abounds today. Man is an enigma, capable of such caring affection and service yet capable of unimaginable cruelty.

I lived for more than fifty years in an old Welsh town with a castle. That building on the edge of the sea can be nothing other than a castle. It is not a bungalow or a shed or a skyscraper. It is a castle, but it is ruined. So it is with man—what accomplishments, what dignity and goodness men display because God has created man. And although sin has ruined him, the God he chooses to ignore and defy—often with intolerable execrations—is a patient, loving God capable of restoring ruined men and women. He has left no one without a witness to His concern for us. He has made us with a conscience. That is the great divine monitor that commends us when we show restraint under provocation, or gratitude when we've been generously treated. "Good!" God is saying, but the voice of conscience also speaks up and addresses our minds, rebuking us whenever we sin. So at this moment you know that besides my words on this page you are hearing another word that comes to you from God. He is urging you to listen carefully to all you have read so far: these are true words telling you exactly who you are—a creature made by God and ruined by sin but capable of being restored by the love of God.

At this point, of course, fears can arise, especially the fear that knowing God and knowing yourself will result in loss: the loss of things that are important to you, the loss of self-acceptance, the loss of your basic humanity. You hear phrases like "being born again" and "being converted," and they seem frightening. Do they mean you are going to lose the very essence of what you are and much of what you know about yourself? Perhaps you have met more than one Christian who has given you the impression of unreality or artificiality—individuals who seem to be less than genuine in their comments, who seem to possess an irritating ersatz kind of happiness.

Knowing God and knowing yourself does not entail the destruction of all you are and all you love.

However, the pilgrimage of your life has brought you to this moment and to this book and its challenge. You have known momentous experiences, great trauma, and now the dawning of a new attitude to God, with all that that might mean for you. But you will not cease to be a unique human being with the gifts and concerns and relationships all real people know. You will continue to influence and be influenced by others and so share in and enrich your basic humanity. Your humanity and identity are not going to be destroyed when you come to a knowledge of the living God. What do I mean by this?

You will still have a unique DNA, your own molecular structure, your individual personhood and temperament and talents in all their individuality. As you come to know God and yourself, your own particular identity is not merged and lost in some vague, standardized religiosity. Men and women who know God don't become as indistinguishable from one another as the images in a little book of postage stamps. Each person eternally will continue to have his or her own temperament. Some days they will be pressed down, feeling discouraged, plodding on with the bare duties of life, hoping to survive, hanging on to God by their fingertips. They will not be ashamed that they don't live in constant religious ecstasy or on a kind of artificial high. There will be winter times when they battle with despair. They will become familiar with grief and disappointment. At times they might feel abandoned by God. But they learn to experience such precious attitudes as real peace, contentment, patience, and submission to God's will. They drink the cup that

God has filled and submit to all other cups being refused. Sometimes that cup is full of astonishment.

Knowing God and knowing yourself is not a matter of your own blossoming natural personality or the sum of the human forces that nurtured you. It is a learning curve plotted by the greatest teacher of all, a growing response to realizing who and what you are and why you are in the world, strengthened by new insights that God provides and a developing maturity.

We may be by nature loud people, restless and discontented by nature, so that occasionally we hurt those who love us the most. We may be bundles of energy, finding it very hard to be patient. We may be easily irritated. We may be painfully shy, finding it difficult to live alongside other people. But the knowledge of God and of ourselves is steadily teaching us how to overcome our sensitivities, providing deliverance from self-centeredness, mocking our vain egos and unpleasing lusts, managing the short fuse of our own irritability, controlling our impatience, eschewing retaliation and resentment, mastering our vices by the grace of God. It takes trust and an understanding of the Lord Jesus to preserve our unique personalities while simultaneously learning to be loving, forgiving, and contented.

You have unique affections. There is a family to whom you belong—spouse, children, grandchildren, siblings, and parents—to all of whom you gladly owe a special love and service. The privileges of family life bring responsibilities. You also belong to a nation. The apostle Paul loved his own people and had a great burden for his kinfolk. He wished that God's judgment might fall on him if in that way his fellow countrymen might be spared. His knowledge of God and of himself had not terminated his national identity. He would always be a Jew, rooted in the attitudes of his own people. Likewise, we do not lose our family, tribal, ethnic, or national characteristics simply by becoming Christians. You bring that to the God whom you have come to know and love, and you challenge and enlighten every human characteristic with the wisdom and love of God. That will deliver you from such follies as making an idol of your family members or having contempt for other ethnic groups.

You have a unique combination of weaknesses. Although you will increasingly know God and who you are, you remain a frail child of dust. You don't suddenly receive a whole new range of abilities through this acquired self-knowledge. You do not experience all your inadequacies being replaced and renewed when you come to know God. You are not suddenly a sportsman, a musician, or the life and center of every group you meet. Some people looked at the apostle Paul and were disappointed in him. They felt that his bodily presence was weak and his speaking was quite contemptible. In other words, Paul had no dynamic, overwhelming presence. Many of his listeners expected a thrilling and inspiring explosion of oratory, but he failed to inspire them. Paul's detractors thought they knew true greatness and true rhetoric, and the apostle didn't measure up. He was born weak both in his presence and in his eloquence, and in their eyes he always remained a weakling. He acknowledges that when he would come to a new area he would speak to people with weakness, fear, and much trembling. He didn't want to get it wrong. He wanted to communicate with the people listening to him and not be bought by their smiles or intimidated by their frowns.

All of us who come to a knowledge of the living God and of ourselves come with weaknesses as well as strengths. One day we may well look back and worship the God of wisdom who granted us such frailties, because those personal weaknesses have kept us casting ourselves on His wisdom. They certainly do not make us fatalists, muttering, "It's the will of God" when things have happened through our own follies. We know that a time came in the life of the apostle Paul when he experienced some necessity and hardship and suffering; he compared the cause of this pain to a "thorn in the flesh." His initial response was not to cry out, "Praise the Lord anyway!" Rather, he took that thorn in his prayers to God. He expressed his grief at this weakness and told God the advantages of having it removed and how much more useful he felt his life could be without it. He persisted in laying this out before God until finally the divine answer came to him that God's strength is perfected when we feel our weakness and know that He alone can help us live with this thorn. Our weaknesses result in our looking to God in trust and asking for His help day by day. The weaknesses of our personalities serve this good end of keeping us clinging close to our God. Our impotence is thus reaching out to grasp His omnipotence.

You have many interests. The God you know has made an astonishing cosmos, from the vastness of the universe to the microworld of the molecule. Knowing God and knowing man does not result in an attitude that henceforth nothing matters to us but the church. If you read the Bible, you find that authors of books such as Job and Ecclesiastes and men like Isaiah and David were interested in everything that God has made, not only because this world belongs to their heavenly Father but also because of its multifarious fullness—that is, its fabric, colors, tensions, emotions, and relationships. Those men were filled with the Holy Spirit as they wrote the Scriptures, and in their books they show that they are aware of such things as music, mining, beauty, agriculture, commerce, fish, children's games, navigation, perfume, politics, travel, medicine, courtship, weaponry, and all matters military. Their vision includes all the dynamics of living in God's creation and the gifts He has given mankind.

The founding members of the church in Philippi were a fascinating trio. Not one of them fit the religious stereotype: one was a woman who had been trapped in the psychic world of fortune-telling and had rejected it at great cost in order to know God personally, another was the Roman governor of the local prison, and the third was an entrepreneur, a woman who traded in purple dyes and materials. All were involved in their world in distinct ways, which led them to be uniquely aware of the needs of those around them.

Our conclusion is that men and women who have come to know God and themselves have a calling to be involved in the world, just as light confronts and transforms darkness. The Christian religion has dealt with vile superstitions and continues to do so. It has spoken up for the unborn child, the slave, the prisoner in a wretched jail, and those who agitate for liberty of worship and expression. Many such Christians have been and continue to be spokesmen who arouse a culture to the evils of ugly and cruel injustices. They refuse to turn blind eyes to such matters, and they ask God what they can do to be healing light and salt in this world.

A number of modern-day theologians, whose fascination has been in the history and teachings of the Christian faith, have also shown their keen interest in everything in God's creation. The man who taught me theology, John Murray, returned from his decades in Philadelphia to the house where he was born in the north of Scotland, and there he spent his last years, not only preaching but caring for a small herd of sheep as his father had on the very same parcel of land. American professor B. B. Warfield, the lecturer in theology at Princeton Seminary, was an expert judge of shorthorn cattle. J. Gresham Machen, the great champion of historic Christianity and founder of Westminster Seminary in Philadelphia, loved mountain climbing. Dr. Martyn Lloyd-Jones, former doctor and preacher at Westminster Chapel, read the medical journal *The Lancet* most Saturdays during the thirty years of his ministry.

Knowing God and thus knowing yourself more fully does not mean the end of your humanity. We must bring all our interests, gifts, and talents to God. We must spread them before Him and cry, "Help me to make these things your servants to be used for your glory and the spread of your kingdom in the love of my neighbor and in doing your will." Yet knowing God does not simply mean an interest in God's creation; the actual mind of the Lord Jesus Christ enormously influences our ways of thinking. How will that show itself? The apostle Paul tells his audience in Philippi, "Let nothing be done through strife or vainglory; but in lowliness of mind let each esteem other better than themselves. Look not every man on his own things, but every man also on the things of others" (Phil. 2:3–4). The mind of Christ shows itself in an utter change of attitude and conduct in relation to all one's neighbors, requiring such an ethical stringency far beyond our natural resources to create and sustain. The Spirit of Jesus Christ creates and sustains the desire to change in these ways, though we generally are the very last people to recognize what God's grace has accomplished in making us the new men and women we are becoming.

THREE

You Could Have
All Your Sins Forgiven

There is a very simple but strong word that is rarely
heard today. It is just three letters long, yet it is a word
that anyone who knows himself and who knows God
must confront: *sin*. A sin is an action against the will of
God that displeases Him, that causes a response of anger
and wrath in our holy Creator, who is totally without
sin. He is light, and in Him is no darkness whatsoever.
He is not indifferent to the activities of the torturer, the
thief, the man who takes another man's wife, the people
who rip off the savings of an elderly person, the man
who is cruel to animals, the suicide bomber, and so
on. God does not silently wink at such activities, as if
to shrug at how some people behave. The alarm bells
that ring in your soul when you hear of such wickedness express a God-given instinctive repugnance at such
actions. Conscience reflects the character of the God who
made us. And we who are made angry at the activities
of the child abductor, the thief, the drug dealer, and the
rapist are also overwhelmed with regret at some of the

things that we have done—how we have hurt those who love us the most and on whom we have most relied. We carry a burden of guilt about our own actions, words, and even imaginations. We are defiled by what we are and what we've done. We are without excuse. If God should give us an opportunity to say a word in our own defense, all we can say is, "I wish it weren't me."

Is there some solvent that can eradicate our guilt? Can we find genuine pardon? Is there any possibility of forgiveness for a person overwhelmed with the pain he has brought on others? Can God remain holy and hating all that is cruel while He simply looks away from the torturer and the tortured sinner with a mere sigh of unhappiness? Would that not compromise His own justice and integrity to respond in such a way?

You might have thought that God is constantly tossing out shrugs of forgiveness, that we murmur to Him that we're sorry and then do some act of penance, and He then looks the other way and says, "OK." Is that what you have always thought in those rare times when you turned your guilty mind to think of God? If so, you don't know God. Our wickedness is a problem to Him. It challenges His integrity, righteousness, and justice. It also offends His love and grace. How would He remain utterly and eternally righteous, condemning all that was contrary to His own nature, and then murmur to a man like King David, who took the wife of a good man and had him murdered, "Oh, that's OK." Such a response would cheapen God Himself. We would then be faced not with a God of eternal light but with a weak and compromising God, one we could not respect, fear, or love.

How can God forgive us for our sins? He could create the cosmos by a word, setting everything in place: the galaxies, atoms, and every living thing. "Let it be" He said, and it was so. However, it was not by a word alone that He showed His mercy. It required sending His blessed Son, Jesus Christ.

After many prophecies that foretold His coming, Jesus was eventually conceived in the womb of Mary, born in a stable, and grew up humbly. He helped His carpenter father in an insignificant village for many years, really tasting humanity and never forgetting its sweetness and bitterness. He was born under the same law of God that we live under. He worshiped God alone, never making an idol of anything. He did not take the name of God in vain. His custom was to keep one day for God each week. He showed submission and honor to His parents. He did no violence, committed no sexual sin, and never told a lie. He did not steal, and He was content every day with all He was given. He never coveted what He saw in others. He loved God with His whole being, and He loved all His neighbors with the same tender regard as He loved Himself. Think of that! As a real man, bone of our bone and living under all the temptations of the world to defy God's sensible requirements, He continued living a blameless human life. He was holy and harmless, a loving person of utter integrity. All of us have sinned and come short of the glory of God, but the man Jesus Christ was without sin. He was also the incarnate Son of God, the Creator, the One whom the winds and waves obeyed, the One who turned large pots of water into pots of wine. He was one who could raise the dead. Here was a human righteousness that was also divine: infinite, eternal, and unchangeable.

This Jesus came into the world to deal with the problem of mankind's guilt in the sight of God. He did this by first living the righteous life that we fail to live and then by giving His life as the ransom for sin, yielding Himself as the sacrificial Lamb of God to His Father. He did not give His body, His obedience, or His human nature. The God-man gave Himself so freely on the cross to which He was nailed. He endured that shame out of His saving love for all His people and was determined to deliver them by making a sacrifice of atonement for the evils that men commit. The very heart of Christianity is that Christ died for our sins. He died as the repentant sinner's substitute so that God remains just and angry with wickedness every day yet shows mercy to all those whose sins have been consumed by His just wrath on Golgotha. Why the cross? Why the death of Christ as an atonement with God? The answer must be that this is how God is. This is His nature. There can be no other way of obtaining mercy. The Lord Christ gave Himself as our substitute, dying in our place.

Do you see what that means for all those for whom Jesus died? All the guilt and shame and blame and condemnation of their sins is no more. It no longer exists. It is as if those sins never were. It is an unbelievable concept, quite incredible and glorious. The sins of those who trust in Christ no longer control or modify their relation with God today. It is as if those sins were not there. There is no guilt at all; there is no defilement. There is only the smile of a loving Father in heaven. God has taken our sin—past, present, and future—and put it all away so that we are as sinless as Christ Himself. He has imputed (that is, laid to the responsibility of the Lamb of God) our sin, but He has also taken that beautiful righteous life of Jesus Christ and imputed that to us. Yes! We are the righteousness of God in Christ. Our sin was laid on the Son of God, and His obedience is reckoned to our account. God remains just, yet He is also the justifier of all who are joined to His Son. We are now whiter than snow and can run into His presence and cry to him, "Father!"

Are you grasping this? I wonder whether your conscience believes it. I'm asking whether you truly and achingly want the burden of your guilt removed once and for all. Do you secretly feel a little sorry for yourself and want to cling in self-pity to what you have been and still are? You would choose that rather than a complete expiation of your liability? Surely not! Let these truths be the whole truth about the way things are between you and God today. There is no barrier at all; there is no impediment. All your sins can be forgiven. Have you come to see it? I pray that this light has shone in your darkness. Jesus Christ has borne all your guilt in His body on the cross. There is absolutely nothing left between God and you, no resentment at all. The single determinant of your relationship with God is what happened on the cross. Nothing else matters.

Nothing else is relevant. Your guilty feelings, struggles, and failures are irrelevant. There are only two factors in the equation: what Christ did on Golgotha and how God responded. I want you to be certain in the depths of your heart that Christ did a proper job of reconciling a holy God to our sinfulness. God has seen the file on you and me; He knows just how rotten people can be. The Lord has experienced their comprehensive rottenness in His voluntary sacrifice and is determined to take sinners like that to Himself forever.

Such love is deep and strange. The immortal died! God gave His life for worthless and self-confident ignoramuses. Such love is past finding out. It is divine. It demands my life and all that I am. I turn from my sin of unbelief and my coldness to God. I turn from all my excuses concerning why I'm not following the Lord Jesus. I run from them, but I run also from the good things that I've done, because in them I will never find perfection. Ego was always mixed with my best words and actions. I have to be "in Christ." I have to entrust myself to Him. I'm not going back to the old ways. They were characterized by too much compromise, hypocrisy, and failure. There was no lasting joy in those things. I turn in repentance and sorrow for my past, and my future is dedicated to living for Him.

What I am saying is that the very beginning of having it all is that we must realize we're not OK. We are sinners who need redemption. We do not receive all that God has on offer by becoming convinced that we are superior to everyone else; rather, we acknowledge that we are no better than anyone else. Instead of believing that we are strong, capable, and competent, we accept that we are prone to wandering, incapable, and weak. It is from this humble place—and only from this place— that we have any chance of growing into the virtues of Christ. We must be able to murmur from our broken hearts, "God, have mercy on me, a sinner." Then, and only then, are we justified, blameless in His sight, and confident in His love. God does not love us to the degree that we are like Christ. Rather, God loves us to the degree that we are in Christ. And that's 100 percent.

It is essential that we begin with this realization— that none of us have the ability to get better apart from the redeeming and restoring work of Jesus in our lives. The first step to fulfillment is acknowledging how unlike Jesus we are. We must not suppress the doubts we have about ourselves. Instead, we must start listening to those doubts and applying the truth about Jesus to them. We must not try to pull ourselves up by our bootstraps. We must not merely think that we have problems. Rather, we must understand that we ourselves are our own biggest problem, our own worst nightmare, our own worst enemy. In one of his messages on the Sermon on the Mount, Dr. David Martyn Lloyd-Jones shares this perspective on our human condition: "The first thing you must realize, as you look at that mountain which you are told you must ascend, is that you cannot do it, that you are utterly incapable in and of yourself, and that any attempt to do it in your own strength is proof positive that you have not understood it."

God's call on our lives, then, is first and foremost not a call to action but a call to brokenness and contrition, for a broken and contrite heart He will not despise. So how do we come to possess all things? We accept the divine diagnosis that our true condition is that of sinners who are bruised and broken by the fall. This may feel contradictory, but the call remains: in the midst of our being fractured and frail, we run from all we are to put all our trust in everything the Lord Jesus is and all that He has done.

Acknowledging our flaws and frailties is itself a mark of grace, a sign of God's kingdom at work in us. From beginning to end, we get all things that are for our good as loving gifts from God. He is the One who begins a good work in us, and He will be faithful to complete it.

FOUR

You Could Become
a Child of God

Become? Surely we are all children of God? If that were the case, then why do you lack this family likeness? God loves His Son, Jesus Christ, and loves the Holy Spirit more than anything and anyone else. This is an eternal and immeasurable love, but only a few men and women love the Son of God today. You must have the family likeness if you are to be legitimate children of our Father in heaven. God gives some people the right to be called His children. Who are they? What have they done? What sacrifice have they made? How did they become the children of God? We are simply told this: they have received Jesus Christ into their lives, the Lamb of God whose sacrifice provides atonement, whose righteousness has been imputed by God to them, and who royally shepherds, protects, and keeps all who have received Him.

Here is a people who have first come to know the God of the Bible and then to know who and what they are in themselves. They have entrusted themselves to Jesus Christ. They have opened their intellects to Him, and their affections and ambitions are now centered on the Son of God. They have welcomed Him into every part of their lives. No part is off-limits to Christ. They have opened up everything to Him. It is to those people alone that God gives the right to be called the children of God.

Every one of these people experiences a new beginning, a new start, a new birth, and it is all God's doing. That is what Christians mean by the grace of God. We become Christians not because of our family's religion or morality, nor because we decided to give religion a go, nor because we were pressured by some religious huckster to make a decision. God changed us from the inside. The new life for those who once were as cold as ice to the Lord is due to His devising and accomplishment; the continuance of our Christian lives into old age and death is also by His enabling and keeping, as is the consummation of our lives in enjoying His presence forever. It is all due to God's grace that once began in us at a certain time, perhaps when we were handed a book like this (or even this book), when a Christian friend we trusted spoke to us and for us, or when we were invited to attend a church where the Bible was believed. Whatever the case, we could keep Him at arm's length no longer, and upon receiving Christ as our Lord and Savior, He gave us the right to call God "our Father who is in heaven."

It was God who made this sweet and gentle change. He altered the relationship between us and Himself; we were once rebel children under His holy wrath, but now we are children of fatherly care. It is God who takes the initiative, just as it is parents who adopt children. There is no way a child can adopt a parent to be his father or mother. An orphan has no authority to wander around a place, choose a big house, and tell a wealthy couple that he has adopted them to be his mother and father and is going to live with them for the rest of his life. The amazing thing about God's adoption is the sort of people whom He makes His children.

Whom do you think God adopts? Your record and future are all known to Him with total accuracy. He has seen the trash, the record of people who have been hurt and destroyed, and the pain you have caused, so you conclude God would never want to give you the right to become His child. You are aware of that, so you suspect you are not good enough; your past is too tarnished. You are even thinking you could never keep up the Christian life, and therefore it's not worth starting.

Those people referred to in the Bible as the children of God, those whom God calls His own, were far from perfect. They were all a mixture of divine family likeness and satanic wickedness, yet God has chosen to be their adoptive Father. Think of King David, the author of the Twenty-Third Psalm, who is described as a man after God's own heart. Yet how does he behave? At times as unlike God as you can imagine. He is a criminal, as cruel a man as many men you would find today in hell! Yet this sad and guilty king grieved over what he had done and pleaded for God to show him mercy. There is scarcely a person in Scripture whose record is not blotted by shameful words and actions. Each one of them behaves just like the leading rulers of the world: they live with many women, get drunk, deceive, kill, allow idols to be erected, are angry, are fearful of threats, and give in to cowardly compromise. They have heard the truth over and over again, yet they reject it and deliberately forget what they have heard. It may be long years before they bend their stiff necks and break their hard hearts.

God adopts people like that into His family. So if you are thinking, "I could never keep walking on the straight and narrow path. I am prone to wander from it. I am a weakling," then the first lesson you must learn is that the condition of setting out as a child of God is that you know your own great weaknesses. You can survive as a child of God only by depending on God's adopting love alone to keep forgiving you, sustaining you, and holding on to you to the end. He will never let you down. He makes rebels and weaklings His children. He did not come to invite just the righteous and good people to enter His family. He is the God of all the people who know their own great need, who have felt the pain of personal hypocrisy and have cast themselves on God's amazing love, saying, "If I die it will be pleading God's mercy in Jesus Christ."

How does God treat those He adopts as His children? We will consider three ways.

1. Their heavenly Father gives them personal access to His presence. A TV reporter was speaking on a live telecast from his home at a tense time in the relationship between North and South Korea. As we watched and listened to him speaking, the door behind him opened suddenly and one of his small children came walking in calling out to him, followed by the child's mother, crawling in on her hands and knees, hoping to dodge the camera's all-seeing eye, then scooping up the pro-testing child away from Dad, who continued to speak to the world of the ongoing crisis! Didn't the child have the right to go to its own father? Of course. Doesn't the child of a president, or a king, or the richest man in the world have access to its dad? Yes, it does. Then this also is the privilege of everyone who has received the Son of God in the glory of His person and in the perfection of His finished work. He or she—old or young, rich or poor, in sickness or in health, backsliding or in the full assurance of forgiveness—can run into the presence of the God before whom the angels hide their eyes, crying, "Holy! Holy! Holy!" We redeemed sinners can burst into His presence, the door never being locked, and can cry out in delight to Him, "Father!" and God smiles in a joyful welcome and hears all we have to say. Please believe me, as astounding as it might seem to you. You can have personal access to the presence of God. You could have it all.

2. *Their heavenly Father provides for their needs.* Any child can expect his father to provide for his needs in a way that is commensurate with the resources at the father's disposal. So it is with our heavenly Father. He tells us to ask Him for our daily bread, and daily He answers every cry of all His children. They sing from

time to time these words, "All I have needed Thy hand hath provided." That is true for them all because God is their Father, and His faithfulness is proverbial. When we shall finally appear before Him, not one of us will protest, "I did not have the provision for my needs. You failed me." None will make a complaint like that. God goes beyond mere sufficiency to provide for all His children very richly, even superabundantly, according to the vastness of His resources. You could receive a divine Fatherly provision for all your needs. You could have it all.

3. *Their heavenly Father protects them from all their enemies.* The duty of a father is to watch over, guide, and protect his children. He always keeps an eye on them, and the younger they are the more he takes responsibility for them. He nurtures and cherishes every one of them as the apple of his eye. Every Christian has many enemies. There is the power of sin in our hearts, which will continue to trouble us throughout our lives. But God makes His home in our hearts when we receive Him, and His Spirit is powerful in striving against our own sinful disposition. We are also under attack from the gates of hell; every little Christian child is threatened by it, but those massive gates cannot prevail against the weakest disciple. They will never lock away forever even the weakest child of God. He has made it impossible for that little one to spend eternity in hell. The enemy of our souls, the devil, goes about this world as its god, always seeking those whom he can devour, but our Father is greater

than all the powers of hell in all their forms of dreadful rage and malice. We have a Sovereign Protector, unseen to our eyes but forever at hand. He is there when we need Him most. He will hold us in His kind, strong hands, and nothing can ever pluck us from that safe place. When temptations come, He gives us strength to overcome them, takes away the desire, or provides deliverance, and He will even use our falls in such a way that the grace of repentance will strengthen us for the future. He will not allow us to be tried more than we are able to bear. Every Christian is kept, moment by moment, by divine personal security. How can you survive without it? Think of it! You could have Omnipotence as your loving protector, eternally faithful to save you, almighty to rule and command your life in love. Do not think of going one more day without Him. You could have the Creator of this universe as your Father. You could have it all.

FIVE

You Could Experience All Things Working Together for Your Good

God is at work in the lives of all those who believe in His Son, and He is working all things together for one glorious end: to make them like Jesus Christ. He has chosen and predestined them to that end. He's at work in their lives making that happen. He has made up His mind to do this. Therefore, anything that makes them more like the Lord Jesus Christ is good, and anything that pulls them away from Jesus is bad.

When Paul says that all things work together for good, he is not saying that the tragedies and heartaches of life will guarantee a better set of circumstances. Sometimes they do, sometimes they don't. God has made no promises about making you healthy, wealthy, and the parent of many children. He is committed to making you like His Son, and whatever it takes to make you more like Jesus is good. In the providence of God, we can learn more in our hours of darkness than we have in the years of light. We could gain more from a bout of sickness than we did from decades of good health. We

pray more when we are scared than when we are confident. As Robert Browning Hamilton wrote,

> I walked a mile with Pleasure,
> She chattered all the way,
> But left me none the wiser
> For all she had to say.
> I walked a mile with Sorrow
> And ne'er a word said she;
> But, oh, the things I learned from her
> When Sorrow walked with me!

What is God doing in the life of every true Christian? He is changing every one of them into the image
of Jesus Christ. God has predestined us to be like Jesus.
Godlikeness is the end of our journey. That's a long road
for us. Along the way are tragedies and many setbacks.
But God will not be set aside, and everything that happens to you—the gut-wrenching grief, the unexplained
circumstances, even the stupid choices you make—all of
it is grist for the mill of God's loving purpose. He will
not give up even when we feel like doing so.

Consider the work of a great sculptor. He intends
to make a beautiful statue and begins by choosing a
rough chunk of marble. In his mind, he knows exactly
what he will do. He predestines that unsightly stone to
become an image of breathtaking beauty. That deter-
mination guides everything he does. He hammers and
chips and chisels, but he won't harm the stone or allow
anyone else to harm it. He will remain at the task until
it is finished. What started as an unsightly piece of rock

becomes a thing of beauty. In the same way, God is at work in your life. Right now you are rough and uncut, and God is patiently chipping away at you. Maybe He's been chipping away at some of you recently. Remember this: He will never hurt you. In the end, you who have received Christ are going to look like Him.

This, I think, is the greatest problem some people have with what I am saying. Their good and God's good are not the same. All they want is happiness and fulfillment and peace and long life as they define these things. Meanwhile, God is at work in those who have entrusted themselves to Jesus Christ, and He uses everything that happens to them to transform them into the image of His Son.

Are you beginning to grasp what I've been saying? All things are included in the "everything" that God works together for the good of His children. We can embrace all that is negative in this life. All those bad situations, in the light of God's powerful purposes, are going to have a positive and glorious end—your eternal good.

This means that nothing haphazard takes place in the life of the Christian. God never shakes His head in wonder, saying, "I never knew that that was going to happen." As individuals we go through sequences of events—some expected, others surprising. We often look at them and see no connection. We ask, "Why did that happen? Why at this time?" But God is the initiator and controller of all those events; He does not merely respond by helping you feel better. For example, when a Christian sins, it is not God who causes the sin or encourages us to sin. God permitted it to happen, but He is not merely involved in trying to remedy a bad situation. His purpose included allowing that person to fall. He permitted Peter to curse and deny ever knowing Jesus. This never justified Peter's sin or any of us behaving badly as we do. We are the ones who have sinned or have suffered because of the sins of others. God cannot be the author of sin, but we are not to regard our sins as things that happened when God was looking the other way or that He was helpless to prevent us from doing. He taught Peter much from his fall and He restored him, using him greatly for the rest of his life.

I have a friend named Derek, and on one wall in his house you will see a photograph of a girl who suffers from a terrible brain malformation. She is now in her forties, though the picture shows her when she was ten. If you ask him who that girl is, Derek will tell you something like this: "From the moment of her birth, and the departure (within days) of her father, who couldn't face the prospect of raising her, her mother has cared for her with undying grace and devotion. As her daughter lives life in a minor key, her mother has found refuge in the assurance that the Lord is sovereign. His overruling providence explains the circumstance she now finds herself in, but it also gives her the resources by which she provides the love and tenderness that she shows each day. The doctrine of providence, of God working all things for our good, is for her more than a mere statement of doctrine, abstract and detached; it is the daily source of assurance that there is meaning and purpose in what is otherwise cruel and senseless." The universe does have meaning, even in the distressing events that happened to the mother and her daughter.

What I am asking you to believe is this: that God uses every obscene evil confronted by every Christian for that person's best interests: death, illness, marital strife, vocational problems, persecution because of belief. In all these things God is working for your good. Your back is broken in a diving accident in a lake. God works it for good. Your husband is having an affair. God works it for your good. Your wife wants a divorce. God works it for your good. Your sister has been abducted, your job has been terminated, you did not achieve the grades you needed to get into the university of your choice. In the book of Genesis we read of how Joseph's brothers sold their own brother into slavery hundreds of miles from home. But what they meant for an evil end, God meant for good. In the New Testament we see how wicked men achieved the crucifixion of the Son of God, but that horror was accomplished by the determinate council and foreknowledge of God. What God purposes in eternity, men will choose in time. God works even the wicked actions of men for the ultimate good of every one of His children. No matter what the circumstances, "God's purposes will ripen fast, unfolding every hour. The bud may have a bitter taste but sweet will be the flower."

You are being presented with this special providence of God's loving care over all His children. You can share in it. I know you may scorn such a claim, kicking against it, but if you do it will be a goad pricking your conscience for the rest of your life. On the other hand, you can have a providential love working all things for your good! You can receive these words as eternally true, the bedrock of all the comforts of your life. You can appropriate this truth, and it will be one of the most enriching promises of your Christian faith, because from it you will learn there is no meaningless suffering in your life. There is no wasted pain in your experience. There is no purposeless event during the totality of your life. God in His wisdom uses every isolated event to bring about your good and His glory.

This is not a new twenty-first-century idea that I have invented to entice you to believe what I believe. Christians have always believed this. Almost three hundred years ago a Christian minister named Daniel Rowlands, who lived not far from where I spent my whole ministry, wrote these words to the people of my county, Cardiganshire:

> We do not say that all things will, but do, work together for good. The work is on the potter's wheel, and every movement of that wheel is for your benefit. Not only the angels who encamp around you, or the saints who continually pray for you, but even your enemies, the old dragon and his angels, are engaged in this matter. It is true, this is not their design. No! They think they are carrying on their own work of destroying you, as it is said of the Assyrian whom the Lord sent to punish a hypocritical nation, "Howbeit, he does not mean this," yet it was God's work that he was carrying on, though he did not intend to do so. All the events that take place in the world carry on the

same work—the glory of the Father and the salvation of his children. Every illness and infirmity that may seize you, every loss you may meet with, every reproach you may endure, every shame that may colour your faces, every sorrow in your hearts, every agony and pain in your flesh, every aching in your bones, are for your good. Every change in your condition—your fine weather and your rough weather, your sunny weather and your cloudy weather, your ebbing and your flowing, your liberty and your punishment, all turn out for good. Oh, Christians, see what a harvest of blessings ripens from this text! The Lord is at work; all creation is at work; men and angels, friends and foes, all are busy, working together for good. Oh, dear Lord Jesus, what hast thou seen in us that thou shouldst order things so wondrously for us, and make all things—all things—to work together for our good?

Again, let me tell you of what could be yours if you receive Jesus Christ into your life as your Teacher, Savior, Shepherd, and Lord. To those people whom God has personally called—that is, whom God has summoned to be His people—all things that come into their lives will work together for their good.

When the apostle Paul and his companion Silas were in prison in Philippi—their backs wounded and bruised and bleeding from the lash, their feet in stocks, in complete darkness—what did they do? They showed they loved God. They showed they were trusting Him and believing that everything they met was bound to work together for their good. What happened at midnight in that stinking dungeon? They sang and prayed, and all in the prison could hear their voices of praise. Plenty of people sing. Seventy thousand Welshmen usually sing some great hymns in a rugby match because of an earlier grace in our principality, but they are not singing those words to God. They will sing them again on the buses and trains going home if Wales has won, but their song is not to a Savior whom they love. A lot of people sing without praying. A lot of people in Wales think that singing is as important as praying, but it's not. I expect at some time the junior Silas turned toward the senior Paul and asked him, "How do you think this is going to work out?" Paul said, "We don't know, but we do know that in all things God works for the good of them that love Him. So let's thank Him for that. Let's pray." They prayed, and naturally they sang to the God they loved. It was a musical night in the prison in Philippi, and the two singers were men head over heels in love with their wonderful God. The audience consisted of all the prisoners, and one could say that the walls, doors, chains, bars, and stocks all clapped when the praying and singing were over. The very stones cried out their Amen! Of course, I am referring to the whole building being shaken when the praying ended. Paul and Silas loved God even when their backs were hurting, and they prayed and sang to Him.

And so it is that God works injustice, wicked magistrates, beatings, scorn, prison, rape, abuse, and total darkness for the good of those who love Him. When the apostle was spending months in prison, he was not frustrated because of his inability to preach and travel and worship with a congregation. He still had God, and so he wrote to the worried Christians in Philippi and told them that what was happening to them all was serving to advance the cause of Christianity. Only a man who loves God could say that.

To another group of Christians who were depressed because of his imprisonment, Paul exhorted them not to be discouraged because of his sufferings. He faced an uncertain and possibly cruel future in prison by kneeling before the Father he loved and praying that God would lift up his downcast brethren. Only a man who loved God could think like that.

If you and I felt what Paul did, we'd never experience another day when worry was victorious or discontentment robbed us of our peace. We would be afraid of nothing. Those who love God know that He is working everything for their good. You could know that for yourself. When Paul came to the end of the journey, I can imagine some of his enemies taunting him, saying, "You'd better get ready. Tomorrow it's the execution block. Head chopping day is tomorrow." Paul would say, "I'm ready now." And when the fellow with the axe came and put the hood over his head, Paul might have knelt down and winked at brother Luke, saying, "I'll see you in the morning. But I'm going home first. It's been a wonderful trip. I've rejoiced in every step of the journey. I just want to say that these words have been my experience all along the way: 'And we know that all things work together for good to them that love God, to them who are the called according to his purpose.'"

SIX

You Could Learn Contentment
in Every Circumstance

Can you imagine becoming independent emotionally, and affectionately, in all the circumstances of your life? You could become content with your lot in life, no matter what that might be. You could become reconciled with your circumstances. That's not to say you escape from them or try to live in a fantasy world, but you can face all that life and death bring to you with totally adequate resources, knowing that you will cope. The Christian is a person at peace with himself, at peace with the world, and at peace with God, whatever situations arise. You can learn to experience peace, trust, and submission in all the changing scenes of life. You can become fulfilled as a follower of Jesus Christ, learning to be independent of your position, your circumstances, and your surroundings. There will be no foreseeable situation in which you need be discontented. Nothing in this world can rob you of your peace. Every Christian without exception can learn this.

This is not a message encouraging fatalism and lethargy. I am not saying, "Just sit back and accept your lot in life." I long for you to change. A child of God wants the whole world to change. The beloved preacher Dr. Martyn Lloyd-Jones once put it like this:

> If you can improve your circumstances in fair and legitimate ways, by all means do so; but if you cannot, and if you have to remain in a trying and difficult position, don't be mastered by it, don't let it get you down, don't let it control you, don't let it determine your misery or your joy. "You," says the apostle, "will come into a state in which, whatever your conditions, you are not controlled by them."
>
> That is what he affirms of himself. "Whatever my condition or circumstances," he says in effect, "I am in control. I am master *of* the situation, I am not mastered *by* the situation. I am free. I am at liberty. I do not depend for my happiness upon what is happening to me. My life, my happiness, my joy and my experience are independent of the things that are going on about me, and even on the things that may be happening to me."

You can gain this attitude if you receive the Lord Jesus Christ into your heart and life. No matter how appallingly difficult your outward circumstances may be, you can become contented, and you have no right not to be. Will you plead your circumstances as a justification for complaining? Would you argue that if I knew what you are going through I would be able to exclaim, "Ah! I have discovered the one follower of Jesus Christ in the history of mankind who is exempt from being contented because his life is so difficult"? Was Joni Eareckson exempt from having to be contented when as a teenager she broke her back and became a paraplegic? What sort of ministry or life would she have had if she had given in to self-pity and anger with God for what had happened? She was not beyond the scope of this marvelous word.

Not long ago in the country of Yemen an Islamic gunman entered a hospital where three elderly American Baptists had worked for thirty years in surgery and midwifery. He shot and murdered them all in cold blood, to the great grief and sense of shame of many Muslims in that district who had loved and respected these kind Christian people. That man has been arrested, tried, and found guilty, but the son of one of the murdered Americans has pleaded for his life, saying, "It will not do any good to kill him." This son is not dominated by bloodlust. That is not his faith. He has lost one of his dear parents, but he has learned contentment with the will of God. Surely in your disappointments and heartaches you too can be contented.

Let me acknowledge one thing so you do not feel overwhelmed. It is not possible to be perfect in any area of your life before glory. Perfect contentment, perfect love, and perfect trust are our goals, but they are unreachable because of our indwelling ego. I know that often we find some thorn in the flesh utterly unbearable. Contentment is something to be learned. It is a process and a progression. In other words, it is not something we are granted at conversion—we are not a restless rebel against God one moment and completely contented the next. True conversion does not immediately remove all the wrinkles in our hearts and souls. Contentment is not picked up in a Damascus Road conversion experience (Acts 9:1–22). You learn it from the beginning of your walk with God. In other words, you read a book like this and learn that God wants you to be a contented person and will help you achieve this. You need not go on in the Christian life disgruntled, with a chip on your shoulder, bitter toward God and your fellow men. You can be a contented person, and most of all, *you can learn how*. It comes as you daily put your trust in the Lord Jesus Christ.

The first principle to contentment is acknowledging that Jesus Christ has been given all authority in heaven and on earth. He is seated at the right hand of God, controlling the universe in all its vastness and complexity. He controls every star in its composition and movement, appoints and determines every planetary system, and determines the qualities of every crystal and chromosome. As Augustus Toplady wrote,

> The fictitious power of chance
> And fortune I defy.
> My life's minutest circumstance
> Is subject to his eye.

Jesus is the One who has scattered a billion billion stars in space; He is the One who gives them all their names. Jesus Christ is the ultimate and foundational entity in this whole material universe.

He is also sovereign over our daily lives, down to the most trivial aspects of our human experience. He numbers the very hairs of our heads and determines the bugs and viruses that give us sicknesses and colds. Knowing that we shall never have any day but a day which the Lord has made is one of the most comforting of Christian principles. Whatever storms may blow, the will of God always presides over our lives. Every day is His workmanship. This is the bedrock of my comfort: that Jesus Christ is in charge of today, just as He is in charge of every day. My life has not been a tale of sound and fury, told by an idiot and meaning nothing; my history has been written by the Savior who loves me. He is the author and finisher of my faith.

He is in charge of the free actions of mankind—of tax officials, doctors, examiners, interviewing boards, soldiers, school teachers, and judges. When they freely make up their minds to work in a certain way, even then my Savior is ruling sovereignly over them. He uses no constraints or compulsion, but their hearts are all in His hands. Let me remind you of how an Old Testament king named Ahab died. An archer far away on the other side of the field, who could not even see the king, drew a bow at a venture and shot blindly into the air before picking up another arrow and shooting that also toward the enemy. He made a free decision. He took aim so hurriedly and shot off his arrow, but God had before planned the place of the shot, the time he shot it, the whole trajectory of the flight, and how its point would pierce a joint in the armor of King Ahab as he stood in his chariot, killing this evil murderer.

Jesus Christ is even in charge of the foolish and wrong decisions men make. At His crucifixion we see Satan attacking, Judas betraying, high priests maligning, witnesses lying, Pilate vacillating, Roman soldiers brutalizing, and a mob shouting. All the world's forces were combining together to murder our Lord, but they were all orchestrated by the Son of God according to the divine determinate counsel and foreknowledge. So it is when men's scorn and murderous schemes are focused on us. They can do only what God permits. When a man named Hudson Taylor went to China, he knew he would meet much frustration and opposition, but he determined to always keep going back to the First Cause. He would look at everything from the perspective of almighty God, who could prevent things from happening but sometimes chooses not to. Taylor refused to be eaten up with annoyance and a desire to retaliate. He believed that if God had decreed that the officials and local chiefs were so awkward, he must challenge himself and ask what he could be learning from this resistance. The Christian believes that when we intercede in prayer, God either gives us what we ask for or gives us something better. That is the logic of our faith in a sovereign Savior.

Nothing can ever happen to me except through Jesus Christ. The preacher of the Sermon on the Mount is in control of my days and my destiny. Gentle Jesus, meek and mild, sits on the throne of the universe and does whatsoever He pleases. Nothing can touch me except what my loving Savior decrees. That is the first means of learning contentment.

The second principle of contentment is being deeply persuaded that this Savior is working all things together for my good. We may make no exceptions when God makes none. The earthquake that rocked the prison at Philippi, the whip that cut into our Savior's back, the kiss with which a mother awakens her sleeping child—all things that touch us must work for our good. Be confirmed that this is so, and when the policeman knocks on your door with a message, or when the telephone rings, or when the doctor's face is grim, or when it is the worst news you could hear, you may know that whatever great changes it is going to work in your life must work for your good. Give glory to God and resolve, with Job, "Though he slay me, yet will I trust in him." There are times when God seems to have become our enemy, but it is only so that He can become our eternal friend.

After all your sleepless nights and heartbreak, His grace will help you to say with David, "It is good for me that I have been afflicted; that I might learn thy statutes." Under all your rejection and loneliness you must conclude, "O the depth of the riches both of the wisdom and knowledge of God! how unsearchable are his judgments, and his ways past finding out!" God usually works for our good by means; by godly, credible living; by the thinking and speaking of His people; by the services on Sundays that we attend. But God can work for our good without means. A man will suddenly turn up in church having never met a Christian. He simply has an overwhelming sense of having to go to a certain church on Sunday.

God can show His power and glory when without means He works for the good of a man. A friend of mine was in a woman's home, in the most compromising of circumstances, and there the Holy Spirit convicted him, drove him out, and began his passionate longing to be rid of his sin and find a merciful Savior. Without using means God met with him, and in the Bible you find men changed by means that you might think would destroy them. God plunged Abraham into the horror of great darkness before giving the patriarch the best light. Jesus put dirt on the eyes of a blind man in order to give him his sight. He refused the plea of the woman of Canaan for a while, arguing against what she so reasonably requested, and all the time this delay was working for her good. I am saying to you that all the paths of God are mercy and that all things work together for good to them that love Him.

The final principle of a life of contentment is to say to God, "Thy will be done." I think this is where contentment grows. We make a commitment in our hearts to this very simple principle: that what I want in my life is the will of my Lord, and as long as I know that this is God's will, I will not quarrel, repine, or be conquered by self-pity. There is no way that we as Christians should say,

"I delight to do thy will, O Lord," and then become upset, annoyed, and plaintive once He gives us His will.

God is sovereign and deals with me always and only through my loving Savior. That's the most fundamental pastoral truth I can make from a pulpit, but when you are down in the valley of the shadow of death, it is immensely difficult. Very often that is the reason we are not content. We do not really like or want God's will. We want to exercise our own will. But I would suggest to you that if we alter our perspective and stand on that principle, "Thy will be done," we would learn many things. We would be taught each day as we rise that it is a day the Lord has made. We will meet nothing but God's will. Nothing can take from us the providence of God. We will have nothing but the cup that God has filled to overflowing.

Do you see the marvel of that? In the book of Psalms in the Bible a psalmist says, "Every day will I bless thee; and I will praise thy name for ever and ever." Each day I am experiencing God's will for me. Every day I am taking the cup He has filled for me and put in my hand. Each day is the Lord's workmanship. When you feel that it's not a good day, say to yourself, "But He has made it."

Do you understand what you could have? There may be tremendous emotional currents running through your life. Your family might be muddled, your friends might be disoriented by unbelief, you might have a serious operation before you, but then, in the midst of your agonies and emptiness you are able to say, "Thy will be

done." Lay hold of this in your desolation: this is the
Lord's will; this is God's cup; this is the Father's hand
being extended to you. And then ask God to keep you
there. Contentment could be yours.

SEVEN

You Could Become an Incomparably Stronger and Wiser Person

Enormous changes take place in the lives of ordinary people who receive the Lord Jesus Christ as their Savior. They are no longer weaklings, wimps, or losers. They do not become fanatics or obsessives. They are given wisdom, and their common sense is greatly increased. It begins when they believe in their hearts the message that the Lord Jesus is the Son of God and begin to live a changed life, following Him. It is more than sixty years now since I became a Christian. One Sunday night in 1954 I sat in a little church (which is no longer standing) in a South Wales valley, and as I heard the message I was assured that what I was hearing was true and that Christ was the Son of God and my Savior.

> You ask me how I gave my heart to Christ,
>   I do not know;
> There came a yearning for him in my soul
>   so long ago.
> I found that all earth's flowers would fade
>   and die,

I wept for something that would satisfy.
And then, and then, somehow I seemed
   to dare
To lift my broken heart to God in prayer.
I do not know, I cannot tell you how;
I only know he is my Saviour now.

—Author unknown

Many things I've done since that night could only
be due to the fact that the Son of God was strengthen-
ing me. He was saving me from despair and the lies of
the devil. He picked me up whenever I fell. He wisely
prescribed for me heartache and repentance. I confessed
my sins to Him. He kept me going. All the good things
in my life were because of Him. Every virtue, every vic-
tory, every confession of sin was because of His power
at work in my heart. When I was poor in spirit, aware
of how dependent I was on Him, it was because of His
might. When I grieved over the people I had hurt, some
of whom loved me more than anyone else in the world,
it was because of His power in me. When my heart was
pure and I hated sensual temptations, it was because of
His power working in me. When I was hungry for a life
of righteousness, it was He who had placed that desire
in my heart and satisfied it. When I came to hate my
tendency to stir things up and to be a troublemaker—to
be a smart aleck, a critic, and a grumbler—He made me
a peacemaker and gave me assurance that I was a child
of God. When I found His cross heavy and my feet

dragged, He gave me power to go on following Him. When His yoke chafed me, His strength made it easy.

The Lord does this to every one of His children without exception, and when we pray for those going through special times of loneliness, loss, and pain, Jesus Christ helps them. That is God's incomparably great power, which all those who have believed on the Lord Jesus Christ have experienced. So we pray for one another that our children, our unconverted family members, the new Christians setting out on this journey, and the old disciples struggling with the weaknesses and pains of advancing years may all know more of Jesus's power working deep in their hearts, souls, and minds. Do you understand what that power is like? It is the working of God's mighty strength that once raised Christ from the dead. It is the same power now living in us.

Christians do not derive their strength from their Christian parents, genetic inheritance, the pulpit from whence they receive the Word of God Sunday after Sunday, their friends, their dear husband or wife, or their personal character. Rather, it is the unique work of the One who raised Jesus Christ from the dead. God raised that dead body to new life. He gave it vitality, power, the ability to speak, walk, eat, and drink. That same power now gives new life to every regenerate believer. There is a presence in the life of the mere Christian that is not of this world. How extraordinary is the being, position, and potential of the ordinary child of God. I am not talking about the gifted Christian, about cultured, eloquent, successful, and honored men of God—I'm addressing all

of us. We sinners who believe in the Lord Jesus are gar-
risoned by the strength of God. Our moral and spiritual
energy is commensurate with this extraordinary work of
God. That Son who once tasted death now lives in us,
and our own power can be measured by the immeasurable power that raised Jesus from the grave.

You could have it all. I am telling you this again
and again because it is true. If you should become a
disciple of the Lord Jesus, you are going to face all the
challenges of this life. You will face every obligation
God lays on His people. You must endure the sufferings of this present time. You must resist the wiles of
the devil. You must love your wife as Christ loved the
church. You must obey your parents in all things. You
must honor your elders. You must be steadfast, unmov-
able, and always abounding in the work of the Lord.
You must present your body as a living sacrifice to God.
You have to face up to the demands of the Christian life.
You are not exempt from one of those obligations. You
could have it all, yes, yet you will confront these challenges with absolutely extraordinary strength.

The "ordinary" Christian is not ordinary at all.
God has given every Christian access to extraordinary
resources, and He expects us to employ this enabling
energy from heaven to be victorious in temptation,
patient in suffering, and submissive in bereavement. In
other words, God requires graces that are commensurate with our union with the Son of God, our resources,
and the glory of our position. The Christian is pressing
on heavenward. He is on a marathon whose finishing

line is the throne of God and the Lamb, and for this race God has made him extraordinarily strong.

I wonder, what is your conception of spiritual power? Religious people speak of powerful sermons, powerful testimonies, powerful preaching, and even powerful worship and singing. They say that the power of God was in such a gathering or in such a life. Yet what is the criterion of power? How do we know the person who is spiritually strong? It is this: being "strengthened with all might, according to his glorious power, unto all patience and longsuffering with joyfulness; giving thanks unto the Father" (Col. 1:11–12). It is not that these men are wonderfully gifted or have superhuman insights, that the gullible swallow whatever their preachers say, or that they are angelic in their manner. It is not that they have power to make people weep; it is not the power to speak with the tongues of angels; it is not that they can command a mountain to move into the sea or perform all kinds of unusual phenomena. A man who is spiritually strong may not know a lot of theology, but because the power that raised Christ from the dead is in him, there is great endurance, patience, peace, joy, and thanksgiving.

You could be a strong person—not strong in having your own way, manipulating people, and dominating your family and friends, but strong in loving, in forgiving seventy times seven, in overcoming evil with good, in turning the other cheek, in considering other people better than yourself, in loving fellow Christians fervently with a pure heart, in loving your enemies. That is real power: it is the strength to be patient, the grace of long-suffering and gentleness, the power to have a grateful spirit. That is what Jesus Christ provides for us, and that is what you could have.

Let me tell you of a Christian woman who did just this. Edith (later Edith Dain) was the daughter of a Free Church of Scotland minister. She sailed to Bombay in November 1935 and arrived at the mission station on December 13, having driven forty-three miles through forest and jungle. After the morning service on Sunday, December 22, she went back to her room with a broken heart. A great tidal wave of homesickness swept over her. She longed to see her father and mother. It would be five years before she had a furlough and could go back to Scotland. The tears were still flowing as she wrote in her diary, "It is Thy perfect will, and I would not have it otherwise. Lord, give me grace and strength not to show this weakness to other people." God answered her prayer, even though the Second World War came and she did not return home for eleven years, by which time her mother and father had both died. She was never to see them again. But the Lord gave her the strength to deal with homesickness while serving far away from her family, friends, and church.

You should know that for more than fifty years I pastored one church in a small Welsh town on the Irish Sea. Of course some strength is needed to preach from the same pulpit for half a century, but particular power is needed to speak a word for Jesus Christ to one person. It can be done only by the energy that comes from abiding in Him.

While I was sitting in the home of my friend and fellow minister, Edward Donnelly, in Ulster not long ago, he spoke to me wryly of our inconsistencies as Christians and especially as ministers of the gospel, particularly of how cowardly he himself is in talking to people he bumps into about the living God. What he said found an echo in my own heart: "If I were invited to speak to a thousand atheists at a great hall tonight then I'd go there and address them all. But do I have the strength to walk across an airport departure lounge and sit next to one man, and begin to talk to him about God? No." So much of what we call power to preach is simply the love of the big occasion and being under the spotlights. Our failure in personal witnessing is that we're not praying for strength to do it. We're not going to God in our desperate weakness to seek His enabling. We are not recognizing that without Christ's strength we can do nothing.

I may face the enmity of a person who can't stand me and misrepresents me, making me out to be an egotist who always gets his own way. How shall I get by? How can I possibly endure all this? When such thoughts arise I must acknowledge that I'm forgetting the resurrected Christ who has promised never to leave me or forsake me. I can do all things through Him who strengthens me. What can separate me from the love of God in Christ Jesus my Lord? I may seem to be poor. I might *be* very poor, and I may be physically and mentally weak, yet who am I? Someone in whom the mighty power of God is at work. The force that made the universe is at work in my life, and every day, despite frequently experiencing heaviness through manifold temptations and moments of anguish and trial, I must recall that this is the greatest of all realities in the world: the dead body of Jesus, bearing the marks of a brutal death, once was laid in a dark sepulchre. Then the stone was tossed aside, the dead body began to breathe, the color came back to His cheeks, the heart of Jesus began to beat once more, and up He stood, alive—never to die again! And I am united to the saving, living power that did that, so I am able to say, "I can do all things through Christ which strengtheneth me." You really could have such strength. Don't turn it down!

EIGHT

You Could Know the Purpose of Life

Can anyone possibly know the answer as to why we're here and what life is all about? There are strident voices that insist on the impossibility of anyone answering such a question affirmatively. Yuval Noah Harari has become a famous best-selling author. He was born in Israel in 1976 and was largely unknown until he published *Sapiens: A Brief History of Humankind* in 2014. Prior to this he had specialized in medieval military history at the University of Jerusalem and then obtained his PhD at Oxford. But in writing *Sapiens* Harari immediately became a publishing phenomenon. It was rapidly translated into forty-five languages, has sold 1.8 million copies in the United Kingdom alone, and has been endorsed by such luminaries as Barack Obama, Mark Zuckerberg, and Bill Gates.

Should Harari be asked about the meaning of life, he steadily affirms the dogmatic answer he gave in *Sapiens*: "As far as we can tell from a purely scientific viewpoint human life has absolutely no meaning. Humans are the outcome of blind evolutionary processes that operate without goal or purpose. Our actions are not part of some divine cosmic plan, and if planet Earth were to blow up tomorrow morning, the universe would probably keep going about its business as usual…. Human subjectivity would not be missed. Hence any meaning that people ascribe to their lives is just a delusion."

The dogmatic assertion of one man's proselytizing faith is that there is no overall purpose to life whatsoever. Life has no meaning; there are only the choices that individuals make—some may be a little better than others, some a little worse—and no one can state that they know that "such and such is the purpose of life." Of course, if our lives have come about simply because of chance over billions of years, one can see the rationality of such a conclusion. If there is no God who created the heavens and the earth, no maker of mankind who has been speaking through His servants the prophets and apostles, and especially by His Son—if all that is a fairy tale and the reason for Socrates, Augustine, da Vinci, Rembrandt, Shakespeare, Bach, Mozart, Beethoven, Dickens, and Einstein is ultimately mere chance—then there is no overall meaning to life whatsoever. We are all living a meaningless existence in a meaningless world, and seeking meaning is futile. As Queen infamously sang in their hit "Bohemian Rhapsody," "Nothing really matters." This is not a debate contained to philosophers; this is in the pop charts. And so we ask this disturbing question: "Is there a connection between such an attitude of life and the wretched choices we make?"

From beginning to end, Scripture claims that God made men and women in His own image. The first chapter of the Bible says, "So God created man in his own image, in the image of God created he him; male and female created he them" (Gen. 1:27). What is the point of insisting that? The point of an image is to capture and display the original—to reflect and glorify it. God made humans in His image so that the world would be filled with reflectors of Himself—seven billion of them, each possessing this one purpose and calling: to glorify, love, and serve their Maker and Provider.

John Piper expresses this well when he says,

> The angels cry in Isaiah 6:3, "Holy, holy, holy is the Lord of hosts; *the whole earth is full of his glory!*" It's full of millions of human image bearers. Glorious ruins. But not only humans. Also nature! Why such a breathtaking world for us to live in? Why such a vast universe? I read the other day (can't verify it!) that there are more stars in the universe than there are words and sounds that all humans of all time have ever spoken. Why?
>
> The Bible is crystal clear about this: "The heavens declare the glory of God" (Psalm 19:1). If someone asks, "If earth is the only inhabited planet and man the only rational inhabitant among the stars, why such a large and empty universe?" The answer is: It's not about us. It's about God. And that's an understatement. God created us to know him and love him and show him. And then he gave us a hint of what he is like—the universe.
>
> The universe is declaring the glory of God and the reason we exist is to see it and be stunned by

it and glorify God because of it. So Paul says in Romans 1:20–21:

> His invisible attributes, namely, his eternal power and divine nature, have been clearly perceived, ever since the creation of the world, in the things that have been made. So they are without excuse. For although they knew God, they did not glorify him as God.

The great tragedy of the universe is that, while human beings were made to glorify God, we have all fallen short of this purpose and "exchanged the glory of the immortal God for images resembling mortal man" (Romans 1:23)—especially the one in the mirror. This is the essence of what we call sin.

So, why did God create the universe? Resounding through the whole Bible—from eternity to eternity—like rolling thunder is: *God created the world for his glory.*

The great tragedy of the world is that while human beings were made to glorify God, we have all fallen short of this purpose and changed "the glory of the uncorruptible God into an image made like to corruptible man" (Rom. 1:23). This is the essence of what the Bible calls sin. We have an insatiable appetite for worship, but we turn from the Creator and worship the mere creature, just as a foolish man with the opportunity of interviewing the greatest sculptor in the world ignores him and falls before the heap of clay in a corner and worships that.

So why did God create the universe? The answer resounds throughout the whole Bible: God created the world for His own glory. He did not create it because He was lonely. He eternally existed with His Son and the Holy Spirit; He had made angels and archangels, cherubim and seraphim. He had no unfulfilled needs, no weaknesses, and no deficiencies. He created in nothingness, out of all fullness and strength and in complete self-sufficiency, out of an overflow of glory and love.

Our calling is not to try to glorify God by improving His glory but rather by perceiving, savoring, and displaying His glory. Stephen was the first Christian martyr, and as he was being stoned to death he prayed that God would not lay this sin to the charge of Stephen's cruel killers. He overcame their evil with his good. Stephen transformed a situation that was not glorifying to God into one that did.

Mary also saw this when she knew she was pregnant with the Christ. She said, "My soul doth magnify the Lord." She magnified God's glory, the way a telescope makes a distant object come closer, bigger, and more real. Our lives are to be telescopes for maximizing the glory of God. We were created to see His glory, be thrilled by it, and display it in our lives to help others taste and see how glorious God really is. In everything we do, whether it is eating and drinking at the table, or anything else mundane, we are to glorify God. As we consider things that are true, noble, right, pure, lovely, admirable, excellent, and praiseworthy, we are constrained to sigh and think, "How great thou art!"

A friend of mine was involved in a debate with an atheist at a university. He asked the atheist how much he knew or how much any of us knew about the cosmos. The man smiled and put a dot on the whiteboard and said, "0.0000000001 per cent." "Then don't you think that in the 99.00000000099 per cent of which we know nothing at all there can be the living God, the God and Father of the Lord Jesus Christ?" "How much do you know?" asked the atheist. "I know little," acknowledged my friend, "but what I know is true and vitally important. I know the purpose of our existence in this cosmos, and I know something about everything that I meet. I know about its origin, that it was created by God. I know about its existence, that it is being sustained by God. I know about its purpose and destiny, that it should be for God and for the glory of the Father, Son, and the Holy Spirit."

What is more important yet, the life, death, and resurrection of the Lord Jesus demonstrates the supreme love of God for pathetic people like us. Our purpose in life is fulfilled when we believe on the Lord Jesus Christ, serve Him, and exalt Him in life, word, and deed. For us there is an unbreakable connection between the purpose of life, the glory of God, the glory of His grace, and the glory of Christ's life, death, and resurrection.

Consider how Jesus Christ glorified God. In Jesus of Nazareth we find a man born and raised in an obscure village, the child of a peasant woman. He grew up assisting His mother's husband in a carpenter's shop; this was demanding yet fulfilling labor. For thirty years He was totally unknown outside that community, but in that place, in the limited pattern of daily life, He glorified His Father, growing in wisdom, stature, and favor with God and the people of that hamlet. He loved His obscure neighbors as His obscure self.

Then for three years He was an itinerant preacher. He never wrote a book, held an office, owned a home, had a family, went to college, or put His foot inside a big city. Except as a refugee from Herod's soldiers for the first couple of years of His life, He never traveled two hundred miles from the place where He was born. He never did one of the things that contemporary society would consider a sign of greatness, but He always glorified God in all He did. On two occasions His Father actually spoke from heaven, commending Him, "This is my beloved Son, in whom I am well pleased."

He was awarded no honors and had no credentials from the powers that be. The religious and civil authorities came to hate Him. He had nothing of this world. When His name became known all over the country, the tide of popular opinion turned against Him. His friends, whom He had cared for so patiently, ran away when armed soldiers came to take Him. The men He loved abandoned Him to them. One of them denied Him and another betrayed Him, but the way He responded to those who let Him down also glorified God. He was turned over to His enemies and went through the mockery of a trial in which witnesses were bribed to lie. He was found guilty and sentenced to death, being nailed to a cross between two thieves. While He was dying, His executioners gambled for the only piece of property He had—His coat. When He was dead He was taken down and laid in a borrowed grave through the pity of a friend.

But the third day God vindicated Him. He raised Jesus from the dead, and for almost six weeks He rehabilitated these people. On one occasion He gathered together and transformed five hundred people so that they knew their purpose henceforth was to glorify Him. They filled the world with their message that Jesus was the Lamb of God who takes away our guilt and reconciles us to God. And Jesus has been filling the earth with His knowledge ever since.

Twenty centuries have come and gone, and today He is still the centerpiece of the human race, the greatest source of guidance and divine inspiration that this world has ever known or will know. Who glorified God more than Jesus? Not all the monarchs who ever reigned, not all the parliaments that ever governed, not all the armies that ever marched, not all the navies that ever sailed, not all the writers who ever wrote, not all the professors who ever taught, not all the musicians who ever composed, not all the scientists who ever rejoiced in their breakthroughs, none of them—not all of them put together—fulfilled their purpose in life and glorified God as mightily as the Lord Jesus Christ.

Here is a man like you and me who possessed neither wealth nor influence yet glorified God in His life. In infancy in Bethlehem He startled a king; in childhood in Jerusalem He impressed theologians; in manhood He ruled the course of nature, commanding winds, waves, trees, water pots, five rolls, shoals of fish, and the sun in the heavens. He walked on the billows as if they were pavement, and He hushed the sea to sleep with a word.

He healed the multitudes without medicine and made no charge for His service. As someone once said,

> He never founded a college, but all the schools put together cannot boast of having as many students. He never marshaled an army, nor drafted a soldier, nor fired a gun; and yet no leader ever had more volunteers who have, under His orders, made more rebels stack arms and surrender without a shot being fired. He never practiced medicine, and yet He has healed more broken hearts than all the doctors far and near. Every seven days the wheels of commerce cease their turning and multitudes wend their ways to worshiping assemblies to pay homage and respect to Him. The names of the past proud statesmen of Greece and Rome have come and gone. The names of the past scientists, philosophers, and theologians are largely forgotten, but the name of this Man abounds more and more. Though time has spread nineteen hundred years between the people of this generation and the scene of His crucifixion, yet He still lives. Herod could not destroy Him and the grave could not hold Him.

He fulfilled His purpose of glorifying and enjoying God, and now He is highly exalted, seated at the Father's right hand. All authority in heaven and on earth is His, and He works all things according to His own will and purpose. He determined in eternity that I would write these words at a set time, words that would help people understand how we could have all that the Lord is offering us. He then brought this book into your hands and has opened your understanding so that you have begun to grasp its meaning and have been given grace to read it to this point. You may have begun to desire what the grace of God alone can supply you. This living, personal Christ, our Lord and Savior, is the means by which we can find the purpose of life and through whom we can have all that God has in store for those who know Him.

NINE

You Could Belong to the Best and Happiest People on Earth

The Lord Jesus called His followers the light of the world and the salt of the earth. They were extraordinary words to address to young men so inexperienced and untried. You can imagine them saying, "Us?" and looking at one another with raised eyebrows. They were being given the illumination of the message of the incarnate God and the power to keep that light shining throughout their lives, which would be like salt, preserving and giving flavor and zing to all they contacted.

What people to be with! Let me find them and mix with them! Let me walk in their illumination and be preserved by their healing protection. Where may I find them? In gospel churches where congregations have received God's gifts of grace.

We need to be with them for our mutual help. Among God's people you will find others who are very much like you: ordinary folk who have come to know God and themselves, who through the Lord Jesus Christ have experienced the forgiveness of sins, who have become children of God, who experience all things working together for their good, who have increasingly learned always to be contented, who have become strong so that through Jesus Christ they can achieve all the things God desires from their lives, who have learned the purpose of life and are pursuing it.

Think of it! You may share in these wonderful discoveries and capabilities with many other people. Who are they? Don't you want to meet them? Wouldn't that be an enormous encouragement to live close to them; learn from them; have their friendship, interest, and prayers; and share common joys and challenges? In fact, you might be able to help some of them as much as they are able to help you.

You will meet such people in a Christian congregation. Without delay, go off and search for a gathering where these truths I've been writing about are valued and taught. Sit with them and watch and listen. It is an essential mark of being a disciple of Jesus Christ that you face up to the privilege and challenge of living with other Christians—with all their weaknesses. You cannot and dare not avoid it. The alternative is unthinkable.

Think of a brilliant soccer player who can dribble and speed past the most experienced opponents. He can shoot extremely powerfully and accurately. He causes his rivals to make mistakes and can read a game and see where the danger is. He is a brilliant all-around player. Yet with all his talents he is modest and prefers to avoid the spotlight. He is one of soccer's covert heroes, yet *he never plays a game*! No one knows of these abilities of his. Why not? He doesn't like to mix with people. He just kicks the ball from foot to foot in the backyard. He watches games live and on TV and sees the strengths and mistakes of others, but with all his burgeoning talents, he never plays a game himself because he prefers his own company. No team profits from his abilities. No crowd shouts his name and cheers his goals. His country's national team is weakened without him. They never win a trophy.

Christianity is a team religion. We are not loners who have become religious but retain the option of being loners. Every believer is put into a body when he or she is given a new birth. We are made by God to belong. If we are Christians, we are in a relationship with, and in the fellowship of, other believers. We need them and they need us. One of the means of growing useful in our families, congregations, and even in the world is by the mysterious influence other Christians have over us. Why go on being lonely?

What can you expect when you start to attend a gospel church? Certainly they will be delighted to welcome you to the congregation. As you continue to attend they will grow in genuine brotherly love for you. They will honor you above themselves. They won't be judgmental about your past or present falls. They will edify you, admonish you, care for you, serve you, and help you bear your burdens. They will be patient and tenderhearted toward you; they will submit to you, just as you will submit to them; they will comfort you;

they will acknowledge to you their own falls and weaknesses; they will pray for you regularly. You need them very much. You can expect to benefit in a rich variety of ways from every congregation that enjoys all the spiritual blessings flowing from our Lord. How can you live without such help? Would a sick man reject every visit to a pharmacist, every doctor's appointment, every stay in a hospital, and all the counsels of a physician? How foolish this ill man would be! Would a child be wiser by constant absence from school and a refusal to be taught, illiterate and disdainful of all knowledge, hating education? No man is an island. We need others wiser and more gifted who are willing to share their understanding with us. We are sheep who need a shepherd. We are novices who need a teacher. We are weaklings who need the support of the strong. We are beginners who need the help of more experienced people.

The Christian life is very demanding. We are asked to present our bodies as living sacrifices to God. We are exhorted to love our neighbors as ourselves. We are to show a forgiving spirit to those who abuse us. We live our lives as sheep in the midst of wolves. We need all the encouragement we can get, and that is why God says to us, "It is not good for you to be alone." He has created this special sanctifying structure—the friendships and support of other Christians in a church—and it is essential for our perseverance and maturation.

In each day of labor for our Lord we are poor in spirit, mourn over our sins, pursue meekness and humility, hunger and thirst after righteousness, strive to be forgiving and merciful people, seek to be peacemakers and pure in heart—it is an unrelenting challenge that ever brings new demands into our lives. Yet we are also encouraged as we see people of like passions to ourselves actually living this kind of life, praying for us, exhorting us, "Go on! Go on! Courage, brother! God is with us! He is our refuge and strength!" They speak like that and live like that. Christian congregations exist in part to keep us going. But you need to be there both to receive and to give.

Remarkable things happen in the church. For example, an acquaintance was helping a fellow member in their congregation to get through a very bad depression. She was suicidal, and he and his friend and fellow leader made a pact with her that she would contact them before she hurt herself. She agreed to this, and one evening she called. She was very low in spirits. They made her promise to meet them at the church that night. They were there to offer her help, and she did turn up, to their relief. They kindly exhorted her, opening up one sweet promise of Scripture after another: how Jesus never leaves us, how the Lord promises provision and help, how we have illimitable access to an indwelling Spirit, how God always makes a way of escape in our trials.

They finally sat in the quiet. They prayed and waited. He remarked afterward, "The spiritual darkness on her was almost as palpable as if it had been a huge dark blanket causing her whole body to sag under the weight." But after several hours, it lifted. There was deliverance. That woman today is a fruitful and faithful member working in her church. She persevered ultimately because the Lord had bought for her that grace. And the exhortations of her Christian brothers that night, by the power of the Holy Spirit, helped to save her. That is a convicting example of why we need to belong to a local congregation of the best and loveliest people in the world. They are there for our good, and we are there for their good. One dark night we may be the ones crying from our hearts to God while our stammering tongues are giving tender words of promise and encouragement to someone with a huge burden. We wait in hope until the darkness is lifted from our friend. Wouldn't you want that? Wouldn't you want your life to count for others? What a wretched lifestyle this life of isolation is! So we need to be with fellow believers for our mutual help.

We need to help each other in our worship of almighty God. Do you find it difficult to worship God in Spirit and in truth? Isn't it one of the hardest things in the world to pray in a secret place? Isn't every source of help in prayer to be welcomed? Of course we must be wise and thoughtful. We have to offer God our worship every day of the week. We read a portion from the Bible and think about its relevance; we pray; we sing praises; we give thanks. That is an indispensable foundation and momentum for corporate worship on the Lord's Day.

We make preparation for worship in good time, starting on Saturday night. We are careful about how late we stay up. It is harder to draw near to God in worship when we are tired. The decisions about what family members are going to wear and what food we are going to eat are all made before Sunday. This will help keep Sunday morning from being a flurry of rushed activity. Then we use our time on Sunday morning wisely; we get up early enough to do everything necessary. We leave early enough to enjoy a leisurely drive to church. We begin to praise God while we are driving. Maybe we have a favorite CD of the metrical psalms or the hymns of Isaac Watts. We comment on some of the beautiful things of God's creation on our way to church—autumn trees, the newborn lambs, the frozen ponds, the heather turning the mountains purple. These simple preparations make us more ready to encourage God's people and receive encouragement from them. The less prepared you are when you arrive at church, the longer and more difficult it will be to get your mind and heart focused properly on the words you are using in the congregational singing, to follow the pastor as he prays, to apply the Word preached to your own hearts.

How many times have you got up on a Sunday morning and said, "I am so tired; I really don't have any energy to go to church." It is the evil one who seeks to influence you in that way, but then you always resist him. You have gone to church and worshiped, and afterward you were more energized to do what you'd heard and ready to offer help to those who had drawn you aside. Sunday worship is renewal. It energizes. It strengthens your trust in God and belief in the promises of Scripture. Martin Luther found corporate worship to be powerful in rekindling his spiritual fire. He said, "At home, in my own house, there is no warmth or vigor in me, but in the church when the multitude is gathered together, a fire is kindled in my heart and it breaks its way through." There are times—may God make them many—when the Holy Spirit takes the reading of Scripture, the intercession of the pastoral prayer, the singing of psalms and hymns, or the preaching of truth and heals us on the spot. We listen not only for ourselves but through the ears of our children and spouses and dear friends in whose midst we sit. We know one friend who lost her husband after four years of marriage, and we can hardly sing the words of a hymn as we hear her singing these words in a nearby pew with assurance:

> Not a burden we bear,
> Not a sorrow we share,
> But our toil He will richly repay;
> Not a grief nor a loss,
> Not a frown nor a cross,
> But is blessed if we trust and obey.
>
> Trust and obey!
> For there's no other way
> To be happy in Jesus
> But to trust and obey.

Children need to see parents participating in and experiencing worship alongside them. The most influential moments in a child's life are often not the moments that parents create but the moments that just happen.

Worship opportunities are filled with these moments. Parents' understanding of worship, attention to worship, participation in worship, and benefit from worship is increased as they are conscious of their children sitting, standing, listening, singing, and praying alongside them in church.

We need to be with others to benefit from preaching and praying. We go to church with the finest and happiest people in the world because the God who indwells and has changed them summons them together and charges them not to neglect those occasions. He desires us to sit with all His people, even the little ones, under the Word of God so that we may be shaped and molded corporately by the Bible. The climax of every service, after we have prayed and sang to Him, is when God speaks to us through Scripture. His purpose is not to shape a bunch of people to be like Christ as individual men and women; rather, it is to form a body made up of Christlike people. We are a body, not a bunch of independent limbs.

When you play a sports video game, you are not on a field with sweaty people running at you. You're not actually there; you are often alone. You don't actually experience what goes on, and it's not really true. It is fake sports. In the same way, when you hear an MP3 recording of a sermon, you're not listening to preaching but to an echo of preaching that once happened in the past. You are in control. You can look out the car window. You can switch it off if it is getting under your skin. Listening to recorded sermons while forsaking the local church is at most second best when you compare it to being there in person with people of God whom you know, those who love you in your local church. It is much more beneficial to listen to the pastor you know and who knows you than to hear a recording of some well-known preacher you don't know and who has no idea who you are.

Do you see the ramifications of physically being in a congregation? One of the main things that comes from being with the local church body is an accountability to one another. Hearing while being together is much better than hearing a sermon alone. The dynamics are different, and we know in our subconscious that the whole congregation is there and has heard the teaching and exhortations. We listened together, we know what each other heard, and then we lovingly hold each other accountable to new knowledge and to the Word coming from the Holy Spirit in power and with much assurance. If I listen alone, no one knows what I've heard. When we listen together, we respond together. The Bible is mostly addressed to the people of God together; *you* is most often read in the plural ("you all"). The Bible's purpose is to make and shape the people of God. So besides hearing God speak to me and asking myself what I learned today, we must ask, "What is God saying to us as His people? What is in this word for our future, for our church?" Don't you yearn to belong to the best and happiest people on earth? You can have the priceless gift of God, belonging for the rest of your life to the family of faith, the body of Christ, God's covenant people, the kingdom of God!

TEN

You Could Have the Assurance That the Living God Will Welcome You When You Die

When the martyr Stephen was dying under a hail of rocks, he had a sight of glory and Jesus standing at the right hand of God. The apostle Paul tells us that he had a desire for his life to end and to depart and be with Christ. While on the cross, Jesus assured the repenting thief alongside Him that the day of his death would be the day he would also be with Jesus in paradise. The dying Christian does not trust in how confident he is but in the truth of the words of the One who said, "I am the way, the truth, and the life: no man cometh unto the Father, but by me."

The Bible says that Jesus Christ "is able also to save them to the uttermost that come unto God by him, seeing he ever liveth to make intercession for them." You see the evidence of that in the gospels of Matthew, Mark, Luke, and John because they all end not in death but in the resurrection of Jesus Christ. He is ultimate reality and is stronger even than death. Consider the dying moments of Jesus. There He was at His weakest, under such pressures to be thinking of His own pain and loneliness, to feel utterly sorry for Himself, to disregard any in need around Him. He who had known no sin was knowing the awfulness of being made sin, the object of the magnificent rectitude of a sin-hating God. Yet in the midst of all this He had time for a criminal who acknowledged that he was justly being punished for his torturous death. If the Lord Christ had time on Golgotha to consider this thief, will He not today think of you, be concerned for you, and change you forever?

Think again of the utter unworthiness of the criminal, the lack of promise, the total lack of potential in the life of this man. The world looked on him scornfully and said, "He is trash; he's getting what he deserves; he's a nobody." At the point of death, what did he have to offer God? This man was not going to be the big Christian spender, supporting the Lord's work for the rest of his life. He was not going to become a deacon, a missionary, or a preacher in the open air. He was simply going to die. He'd never come down alive from that instrument of torture. Yet with nothing at all to offer God, he received mercy and was saved.

Surely if salvation is of grace and not of works, you see it in the compassion of Christ's final moments. The thief was never baptized, never took Communion, yet his heart and life were moved by the dying, loving Jesus, and the Savior heard his few words, ignored his vast ignorance, and saved him. Thankfully the way of salvation never changes. He who saved the dying thief lives and is with you today as you read this.

The dying thief rejoiced to see
That fountain in his day,
And there have I as vile as he
Washed all my sins away.

Dear dying lamb, Thy precious blood
Will never lose its power,
Till all the ransomed church of God
Be saved to sin no more.
　　　　　　　　—William Cowper (1731–1800)

How near a person who trusts in Jesus Christ is to heaven! The moment a man believes on the Lord Jesus alone for salvation, his place in the presence of God is secured. His eternal position and state is settled at the right hand of God with his Lord. No other may take his place, and he cannot lose that place. He has entered his eternal kingdom already. He is under the government of its King. Jesus says to this man, "Today shalt thou be with me in paradise." There's a body of divinity in that phrase. "Today," says Jesus. In other words, in Christ you are ready to enter God's kingdom. Let me put it this way. If you have put your trust in Jesus, you are as ready this moment sitting in a chair and reading these words as you will be on the moment you will breathe your last. You are as ready as if you had served and suffered for Christ as the apostle Paul had. You are as ready for a glorious entrance into heaven as anyone whose faith is in Christ. If your faith is as thin as a spider's thread, as long as it is lodged in Christ you are safe. It is not great faith that makes us ready for heaven, it is a great Savior who saves us through faith in Him alone. Our future glory depends not on the best works we have done but on God's delight with the Lord Jesus and His perfect works. For Jesus's sake God washes us and takes us to Himself. It is His joy to open heaven for all of us.

> The thief who near the Saviour hung
> (In death, how happy he!)
> Was answered when his dying tongue
> Said, "Lord remember me."
> My sins are not less black than those
> Which brought Him to the tree:
> No thought can give my heart repose,
> But Lord remember me.
>
> —John Newton (1725–1807)

What a wonderful day it was in the life of the thief on the cross. That morning he breakfasted with the devil on earth; that night he supped with Christ in glory. That morning he was a culprit standing before the bar of earthly justice and was found guilty; that night he stood before the bar of divine glory and was justified. That morning he went out of the gates of Jerusalem, hooted and jeered and pelted; that evening the gates of the heavenly city opened wide and an innumerable company of angels rejoiced at his entrance. Jesus, who actually died before him, was there to welcome him and introduce him to His Father. It all happened on that wonderful, marvelous day.

Oh, that today might be such a day for you! The set time, when God has dealt with you in Christ, when you come acknowledging your own sin and need, seeing in Him an all-sufficient Savior—may it be today.

Conclusion

You could have it all. I have given you the warrant to believe the extraordinary possibility that all this could be so, however wretched and indifferent your life has been toward God until today. All that I have written to you could actually become yours. Think of it:

- You could know God.
- You could know yourself.
- You could have all your sins forgiven.
- You could become a child of God.
- You could experience all things working together for your good.
- You could learn contentment in every circumstance of your life.
- You could become an incomparably stronger and wiser person.
- You could know the purpose of life.
- You could belong to the best and happiest people on earth.
- You could have the assurance that the living God will welcome you when you die.

Please understand me. I am not saying, "I guarantee all this is yours." I am making a crucial distinction. All the above is being offered to you today, but it is not being promised to you simply because you have read these words. I don't promise this to all who have casually read this little book and still say, "Yes, but…." If you are still uncertain and indifferent, I am not promising you that all is well and all is yours.

All the above is being promised only to those who turn from their unbelief and put their trust in Jesus Christ alone for salvation. If you believe that He is Lord and you want Him to become your Savior and Lord from this moment on, I promise you that you will have all I have written about. All these inexpressible realities can become yours—truly, infallibly, effectually, eternally, and quite freely at this very moment. In this book you have encountered the free, unembarrassed, and sincere offer that God is making to do all of this for you and in you. There is no more to find out. Do not trifle with your soul's salvation. God has been speaking so kindly and lovingly to you concerning what He is freely offering you today. The price of receiving all of this has been paid for by the life and death of the Son of God. He has bought these blessings for all kinds of sinners just like you. He is offering them to you. Take them! Taste and see that almighty God is good. Do not tarry. Receive the loving Christ as your Lord and Savior now. Believe it. It is true. There is no better reason to receive all this. It is truth, and it can be yours as you receive it by trusting the Christ who cannot lie. Think of it—you could have it all.